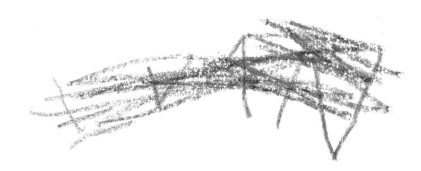

Zebra Sharks

by Nico Barnes

ABDO
SHARKS
Kids

www.abdopublishing.com

Published by Abdo Kids, a division of ABDO, PO Box 398166, Minneapolis, Minnesota 55439.

Copyright © 2015 by Abdo Consulting Group, Inc. International copyrights reserved in all countries.
No part of this book may be reproduced in any form without written permission from the publisher.

Printed in the United States of America, North Mankato, Minnesota.

052014

092014

THIS BOOK CONTAINS
RECYCLED MATERIALS

Photo Credits: Getty Images, Shutterstock, Thinkstock, © Matthew Field p.1 / CC-BY-SA-3.0

Production Contributors: Teddy Borth, Jennie Forsberg, Grace Hansen

Design Contributors: Candice Keimig, Laura Rask, Dorothy Toth

Library of Congress Control Number: 2013952580

Cataloging-in-Publication Data

Barnes, Nico.

 Zebra sharks / Nico Barnes.

  p. cm. -- (Sharks)

ISBN 978-1-62970-069-4 (lib. bdg.)

Includes bibliographical references and index.

1. Zebra sharks--Juvenile literature.   I. Title.

597.3--dc23

                 2013952580

Table of Contents

Zebra Sharks

Zebra sharks live in the Indian and Pacific oceans. You can find them in warm, coastal waters.

4

5

Zebra sharks prefer shallow waters. They like having places to hide and rest.

Adult zebra sharks have

spots on their backs.

They are sometimes

called leopard sharks.

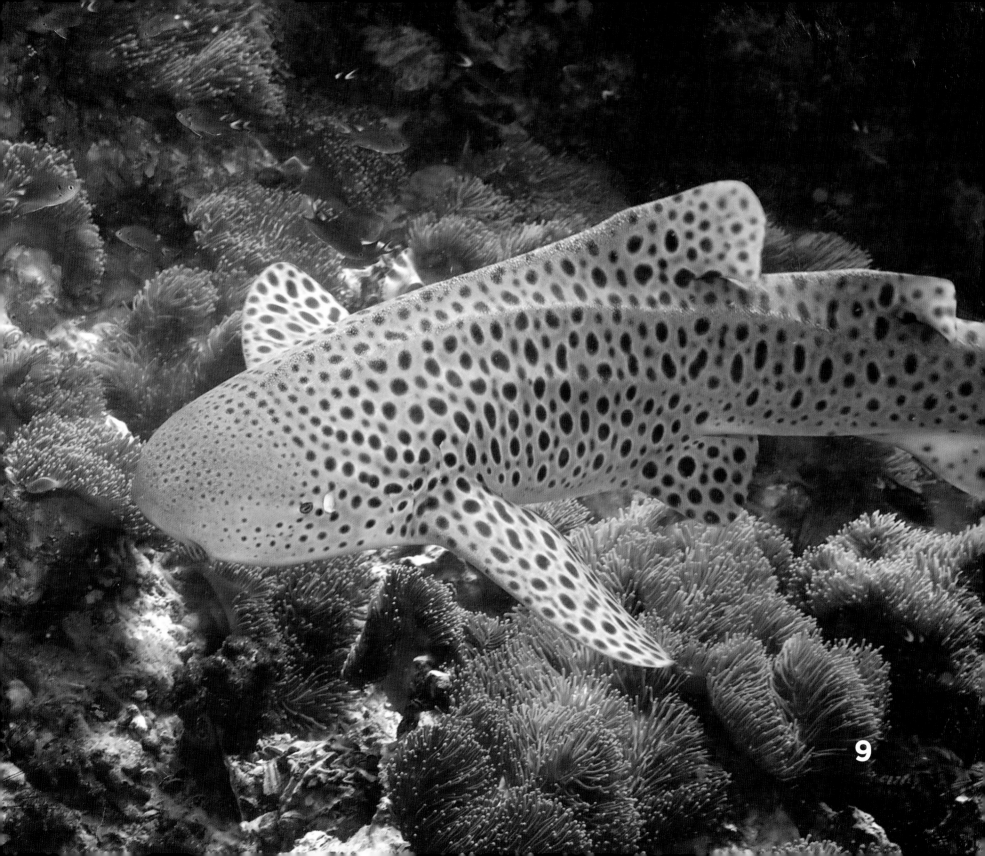

9

Zebra sharks are long and flat.

They lie flat on the ocean floor.

11

Zebra sharks have long tails.

Their tails help them to swim.

13

Zebra sharks are slow swimmers. They swim a lot like **eels** do.

14

Hunting and Eating

Zebra sharks hunt mainly at night. Their favorite food is fish. They like crabs and snails too.

16

Baby Zebra Sharks

Zebra sharks lay eggs. They lay about four eggs at a time.

Baby zebra sharks are called **pups**. They have stripes when they are born. Pups are on their own after they hatch.

More Facts

- Zebra sharks are nocturnal. That means they sleep during the day and are awake at night.

- Zebra sharks have few **predators**. Their biggest worry is larger sharks.

- A zebra shark's mouth is designed to crush the shells of some of its **prey**, like lobsters, oysters, and clams.

Glossary

coastal – near land.

eel – a long, thin fish
that looks like a snake.

predator – an animal that
lives by eating other animals.

prey – an animal hunted
or killed for food.

pup – a newborn animal.

shallow – not deep.

Index

abdokids.com

Use this code to log on to abdokids.com and access crafts, games, videos and more!

Abdo Kids Code:
SZK0694